THE JOURNEY
AND OTHER POEMS
MAHMUD KIANUSH

Newton-le-Willows

Published in the United Kingdom in 2020
by The Knives Forks And Spoons Press,
51 Pipit Avenue,
Newton-le-Willows,
Merseyside,
WA12 9RG.

ISBN 978-1-912211-71-5

Copyright © Mahmud Kianush, 2020.

The right of Mahmud Kianush to be identified as the author of this work has been asserted by them in accordance with the Copyrights, Designs and Patents Act of 1988. All rights reserved. No part of this publication may be reproduced, stored in a retrieval system, transmitted in any form or by any means, electronic, photocopying, recording or otherwise, without prior permission of the publisher.

Other books in English by Mahmud Kianush

Editor and translator:

Modern Persian Poetry

Poetry

Of Birds and Men: Poems from a Persian Divan
Through the Window of Taj Mahal
The Amber Shell of Self
The Songs of Man
Poems of the Living Present
Thorns and Pearls (Bilingual)

Contents

Foreword	7
She Is a Tree	12
Tchio, Tchio!	13
I and the Body	15
Light and Pure	16
Spider and Fly	17
Poems Reincarnate	19
Take It Back	21
A Footnote	23
O, You, the Sun	25
Awesome	27
The Journey	28
The Game	30
The Meaning of Life	34
We, Our, Ours	46
Nothing Is Eternal	50
To Lila	64
Genesis III	66
Blessed Are the Wolves	68
Suddenly	70
Amusement	72
Now in Silence	73
These Stars	74
Perhaps the Earth	76
It Is only the Wind	77

We Are Going Far Away	79
And this Blind Rat	81
Market of the Day	83
No Pretensions	85
Now See It as …	91
Oath	93
Evening of Togetherness	95
Anyhow	97
Thou Art Thine Cosmos	98
Perhaps	102
The Blossom of Astonishment	104
Zubaida	120
At The Green Gate	128
What Do We Think of the Birds	134
Her Words	135
And He Will Die with Me	136
Ode to the Truth of Being Human	138
About the Poet	145

THE JOURNEY
AND OTHER POEMS

Foreword

The time has come for us humans
to free our God from the prison
we have made for Him
              with our primeval illusions,
no matter how innocent
              our original intentions were;
and let Him return
              to His realm of unknowability,
with no absurd desire
              for being known by us
whom,
    we think,
        He chose
            to make in His own image.

Now it is time
            for us humans
to stop worshipping a strange god,
essentially
        and wholeheartedly
familiar to this speck of dust
              which we call the Earth,
but absolutely alien
              to the infinite Universe,
which He supposedly created
for no other purpose
              but to give a fantastic look
to the lofty dome of our sky
on calm
      and clear
           nights.
Now it is time for us humans of today,

to let History retake
                its real status
and remain
        and act
as the dutiful chronicler
of our past struggles,
            mistakes,
                    and illusions.

Come,
      let us exorcise History
                    from our blood,
so that we can breathe
            the air of our real Time
in our real Environment;
so that we can watch,
with our fresh,
        unlearned,
               prehistoric eyes
the fascinating,
but cruelly disturbing nonsensicality
of the non-stop,
            intoxicating show of life,
with all its hilarious mating festivals,
all its virile beauty power contests,
and all its eat-and-be-eaten makeshift banquets!

Come,
     let us watch any
            and everything
in such a manner
as if nothing existed
            before we found ourselves
conscious of being
        and of being here,

faced with a "Something"
that doesn't answer
                          to our perplexing questions,
and makes us silently shout
from the depth of our conscious being:
"What the hell,
            Or, the paradise,
                          is it all for?
If it all is nothing but
                the wild dream
                              of an Anti-God?"

Come,
      let us grow up and out
                    of our childhood
which we have been dragging with us
since the start of our self-exile
from the garden of wild innocence,
like an invisible tail,
but heavier than the pain of our sufferings,
and longer than the length of our endurance.
Let us gather
         all the beautiful and lulling tales
said,
    sung,
           and immortalized
                       in *biblia sacra*
by our far ancestors,
and bury them
            with all due respect
in the golden domed museums of antiquity,
and come out of this lullabied trance
as real awakened adults,
and clear our memory
of all the tribal toyish idols;
of all the truth-fearing

                    sanctified heroes;
of all the singing words,
insincerely gilded
                    with divine delusions,
for nothing
            but earthly gains.
It is time for us
to rise and stand
                    as tall as the sun
at the feet of
            the glorious adulthood
of the enlightened human race,
with a new generation of apostles
whose messages come from their meetings
with the inner reality of things,
as the gradual stages
of their perpetual journeys
in search of some convincing signs
of a meaningful,
            existential
                        relationship
between the will of the conscious self
and the will-less organic life
                        of growth and decay,
to ultimately attain
the absolute tranquility of Truth.

It is time for me
to call my fourscore years of
   rest-
      less-
         -ness
            on
               Earth
"The Undestined Journey of A Gypsy:"
The gypsy of the Universe,

                                                    Man,
ever-wandering,
not in search of the mystery of the "Self,"
but in watching the expanse
                of "Consciousness."

And now,
The wandering God:
– The speck of Dust,
        The drop of Water,
                The breath of Fire,
                        The ray of Light,
                                All in One –
Is retiring in Peace,
Out of the domain of Time,
For a quiet Homecoming
                to the Unknown.

She Is A Tree

She is a tree
Of a pure ancient origin;
She has six lovable branches,
One of them standing out,
Not in size,
            in shape,
                        or in colour,
But because this branch of hers
Is blessed with the exalted nest
Of a unique bird
Who has song messages
From the Unknown.

6 March 2014

Tchio, tchio!

It may take you a few minutes,
Or, if you were I,
          many years
To, at last, realise that
Passing through
          the green corridor
                    of birds,
Your distorting imitations
Of their eternally perfect songs
Can confuse their peaceful instincts;
Can make them suspicious
Of an intrusion of the unknown;
And put them into the silence of fear.

After many years
          of misconception,
At last, I realised
That I should stop abortive deception
And humbly try to find
          my own song,
Something artless,
Something simple to remember,
To repeat with natural precision
In almost equal intervals.

Today,
Passing through
          the green corridor
                    of birds,

I tried
    my meticulously performed song:
"Tchio, tchio! ... tchio, tchio!"
I think, I was cautiously welcomed
                              as another bird.

I and the Body

Not complaining
           of the absurd Reality,
But to simply let her know
My pure feeling of the moment,
I said to her:
"My worn-out body
           is in agony,
But I still possess
My smile of endurance!"

Two aliens,
One in appearance
And disappearance
           here,
Namely Earth,
The planet of Life,
       Beauty,
              and Wonders;
The other,
     "I,"
        the exile,
Suddenly thrown
           down here
From no one knows Where,
To dwell inside the Other One,
To grow into a thinking mirror
Reflecting the infinite Universe
With the invisible face of God,
And then…
And then
       Nothing!

2 April 2014

Mahmud Kianush

Light and Pure

Now,
        at last,
I am leaving behind
All the darkness;
Now I have all the light
               I need
In my head,
In my eyes,
       and in my heart.

Now
I am passing through
A pearly
     mythical
          mist,
With the scent of milk
And the taste of honey.
It mixes with my breath,
And flows into me,
Cleansing my blood
Of all the impure
           and dark memories,
Memories of false creeds,
Of sins and punishments;
Memories of inhuman deeds,
Of history and its facts.

Now I am freed
From the curse of darkness,
I am as light and pure
As the sacred Nothingness.

9 April 2014

Spider and Fly

Yes,
When I was still sinless
And lived among the innocent,
I was not yet afflicted
With the malaise
          of doubt,
With the mania
          of having questions;
I did not know who I was,
And did not need to know
              why I was there.

I was there
And it was good
          to be there,
It was pleasant,
And full of enjoyment,
Though not all the time!

I was my feelings,
And my feelings were my world,
And my world was free from meaning;
I was my time
        and my space,
I was all!

I was all
      before my separation
             from the space,
Before being turned against
              by time,
And left lost in despair.

Yes,
I was happy then,
When I was sinless,

Living among the innocent,
As is now,
One of them,
This tiny Spider
In the dark,
       damp corner
Of this tiny toilet
           in the back garden,
Looking with joy
       at a fly
Tinier than itself,
Fallen victim into its tiny web!

Yes,
Now I know it well
Why I did not want to be sinless
And to live with piety
Among the innocent.

13 April 2014

Poems Reincarnate

You are right:
Poems reincarnate,
Or, in other words,
Poets are the faithful descendants
Of the creators of meanings,
The musing humanizers
Of the world of appearances,
The myth makers,
The first Adams and Eves,
In the first era after the Fall
                        to elevation,
Out of the Paradise of the Mute.

And the Lord God brought
all the wild animals
and all the birds in the sky
                    to the man
to see what he would name them;
And whatever the man
       called each living creature,
              that was its name.

Yes,
    but not so quickly,
                so impulsively,
And in such a haphazard way!
For naming animals and birds,
    [and before them,
               perhaps,
    plants and trees,
    herbs and flowers,

and after them,
                    perhaps,
        the fish and other sea creatures],
Adams and Eves
First looked,
For long enough
                at each one of them
In the mirror of their own feelings
To see if they were in harmony
                            with their life,
Or hostile and harmful to it.
And then,
With all their love
            or all their fear,
They created them again
In the images
            of their human experiences
Which now
            really existed
And were intimately known
And named and remembered
                    in metaphors.

All the nouns
        were originally metaphors
Made by Man,
The Poetical Animal,
The Creator of the World in Words.

20 April 2014

Take It Back

I was an angel
  and heavenly paradise was my home,
Adam was the cause of my fall to exile
  to this abode of dust and destruction.
        – Hafiz of Shiraz

Take it,
Take it back,
            and burn it,
And pulverize it,
And let it be merged
                again
With the infinite absurdity
Of your divine inertia.

Take it back,
Take it away from me!
It has always been wild,
                wild,
Wild and untameable
                as hyena,
And always in hunger
                for flesh.
By its essence
It began to smell of rottenness
From the very first day
Of the atonement.

I have tried my best
            to get used
To its hideous habits,
But to share
            his enjoyment of them

Is,
    and always has been,
More than the negation
              of what I am
In my own essence!

In my own essence,
I am an alien here,
From the Planet Thought,
Of the Universe of Words,
Always wondering
If I shall ever know
What is
      The Why of It All!

O, The O,
        The Big O,
Thy own praise be upon Thee!
I am not the Flesh,
I am the Meaning;
I manifest myself
            in my arts
                and my words;
This rotting bundle of pain
Is not my habitation;
Take it back,
Take this curse away from me!

27 April 2014

A Footnote

Perhaps,
When you *"drink the sun"*
In the *"raindamp grasses,"*
You have a consoling message
From the hot spring of your heart
To that selfless furnace
Of hydrogen,
        helium,
                and of life.

Perhaps,
When you feel
        you have so ravenously
This savage desire of *"devouring,"*
Whatever it is that you love,
The self within
        makes you wary
Of the world without
Through the pain of experience,
The pain of the dead memories,
Deeply buried
In the dark ruins
        of your time past.

Perhaps,
When you become *"a river,*
Reaching out in every direction,"
With your *"watery hands"*
In need to *"find and hold"* the "other,"
This is for you
Another way of committing to paper

Your odyssey of self-attainment:
Looking into the right mirrors
To see the living reflections
Of your own thoughts and feelings,
While enjoying the purity of life
As being lived by a finch
              with a worm in its beak;
A playful rabbit chased by
Its very merry mate
              across a wheat field;
Or a butterfly,
       with its wings in full array,
and so still as if
          pinned on a rose leaf.

Perhaps …
No!
Let me be brief and say:
"Love thy own self,
          and thou wilt love all!"

O, You, the Sun

We are clouds,
Clouds,
The fellow-travellers of the wind:
And our Life is
The manifestation of our restlessness;
Wherever grass and flowers
                          grow on earth,
They are our travel diaries
On this destined,
               but blessed journey.

O, you, the eea!
For the present
I have nothing to say.
You know very well
That in the very end
Outside your great womb
There is no path
               to any destination.

Be there,
      as yourself,
             you the sea;
The traveller,
      now tragically tired,
Is on his way,
      coming.
The journey will soon come to its end.

Until the time
               when I,
                       again
Will give my heart
                 to the pure silence,
And again
The dreamless,
            heavy sleep
                      of oblivion
Will take me in her arms,
Here I am
          with the blitheness of love,
Full of the passion of light
And divinely aware of existence.
Harken!
O, you, the Sun.

Written in Persian in 1986,
published in a book titled *The Book of Friendship*,
in London by Shoma Publications;
rewritten in English for my friend and daughter-in-poetry,
Joanne Arnott.

22 September 2014

Awesome

*The People long eagerly for just two things –
bread and circuses. Juvenal, Satires*

We were in the pharmacy again.
He let out a tired smile,
And closing his dripping umbrella,
                         he said:
"Awesome weather,
            awesome!"
Tiredly smiling at him,
                I said:
"Awesome,
       and also awful,
The weather,
And many, many other things,
But, nonetheless,
            we can feel happy
Because before the followers
Of any religion
          can ever prove
The existence of their deity,
We all can prove
The humanness of our Being,
Not by worshipping,
But by living like a God."

13 October 2014

The Journey
For Enayat Fani

Long,
       too long,
And packed with unexpected perils
Was this unplanned journey
On which I set out
In a moment of ennui
As if impelled
          by a mighty impulse.

Do I regret my instant decision?
No,
    not at all,
Because in that moment
The only way to free
          my conscious self
From the absurd state of life
Was to rebel,
      to run away,
To leave behind
         the inertia of resignation.

But to make it meaningful to myself
I called it a journey of discovery,
Which is in itself
A motion towards the Unknown,
With no direction,
         no destination,
And utterly devoid of guidance.

Now
Tired,
  tired,
    tired,
And
Unashamedly disinterested,
I stop here,
At this point of the journey,
And,
Giving a compulsory respite
To my burdened memory,
I cut my conscious connections
       to everything,
To all and everything
I have seen,
  and thought,
    and done
Since that exploding moment of ennui,
And woe and behold,
I feel I am exactly where the journey began.

Then and there
I felt lost and lone among the others;
Here and now I have found
      my Alone Self
In the infinite domain
    of Eternal Lostness.

14 November 2014

Mahmud Kianush

The Game
For M. H. Sabahi

He is young enough
                    to be my grandson:
It was our second meeting,
And we were supposed to play
                            backgammon;
But looking into my eyes,
                        I think,
He saw something in me
That made him shudder in his mind.

I was a single flake
                of a rare snow,
Coming from the heaven
Of Thought and Beauty,
Fallen gently,
            by pure chance,
On the open palm of his hand,
A hand healthily warm;
Warm
      with the forceful love of life,
Warm
      with the holy desire of truth,
Warm
      with the graceful courage of doubt.

He gave a silent sigh of regret,
As if he was watching me melt away,
Evaporating into the dark of the void.
He deserved to be saved
From whatever it was
That had made him sad,

Or distressed,
     or apprehensive,
          or frustrated
               with senseless regret.

Pointing
     to the unopened backgammon box
Laid on the corner of the table,
               I told him,
With the smile and the air
          of a grandfather:
"Let us not forget the game;
Let us play as we think and talk;
Let life take its own time and pass."

Now we opened the backgammon box
Which was last closed
          and put away
More than,
     perhaps,
          thirty years ago
When I had finished
          my last game
With my own son
Who has been living since then
In another,
     but not too far, country.

My young friend.
– Companion in thought and play –
Needed something to help him let
His distracted mind regain
Its youthful,
        clear,
            brightness.

I remembered that once,
                      long, long ago,
I needed a symbolic metaphor
About the mystery of life
By which to console a friend
Whose grandfather had passed away:

"You see, my friend,
There lies the ocean of life,
Probably whole and indivisible;
And suddenly,
A playful, invisible wind of change,
Somewhere,
                on the surface of the mystery,
Jumps up and begins to walk,
And dance,
        and whirl and swirl and run:
It is on its footprints that rise,
Here,
     tiny ripples,
With the jingle of humble sighs;
And there,
        mountainous waves,
With the volcanic arrogant eruptions.

Waves or ripples,
                whichever we be,
We rise and fall
And the ocean remains
Always,
     always the same:
Whole and indivisible!"

We had set up our checkers,
And my young companion
Who had the dice in his hand,
Was waiting for me
To finish my words of consolation.

He smiled a smile,
                not of relief,
But of despair,
                and said:
"If it be so,
        it is absurd and cruel!
I cannot deny its reality,
But I'll always stand against it!
Rise and fall,
        and nothing else?"

And I smiled a smile
                of understanding
                              and said:
"Let us play, my friend!
The ripple of light is still here,
Here,
        on the apathetic ocean of darkness;
Let us play and forget
Until the time comes
For my playful wind
                to be extinguished."

23 November 2014

The Meaning of Life

For Ugis Praulins, my composer friend,
And his beloved Inga.

i

Her young son,
Who has recently turned eighteen,
Has been afflicted with doubt
About the essence of happiness
And the meaning of life.

It was a disturbing,
                unexpected question
Put to a mother
By a son whose faith in motherhood,
In his turbulent stage of life,
Was,
    somehow,
Greater than his love for his mother.

The strange flow of numbness
Which took over her mind,
Penetrated her tongue
And kept her silent for a long moment
Until the question came again,
This time
        with the impatience of despair.

The welled-up,
        but held-back,
               tears
Made her eyes shine
        with a sad light.

Her numbness changed
To a forceful emotional excitement;
Sitting close to him,
She hugged him,
        and patted his head,
Caressed his hair,
        and kissed his hot forehead.

The boy let his mother do to him
What a little girl might do
To her lifeless doll
As some owed loving apology,
Without being comforted
With any appreciative gesture.

Now the mother,
Her consciousness divided
Between the past and the present,
Began to search in the attic
        of her memories
for the left and forgotten pieces
Of an uncomposed treatise
Which she expected to contain
The basic elements
        of a general answer
To the eternal questions:
The meaning of life,
And the essence of happiness:

"You see,
        my dearest darling son,
When I was,
        like you,
In my late teens,

I began to have doubts,
Doubts about many things,
Above all,
About the real meaning of life,
And the essence of happiness;
But, you know,
        my son ... "

ii

She,
    the mother,
Fifty-five years old,
Admired by her friends
For her courage
        and self-reliance,
For the first time in her life,
Found herself challenged
By a great failure
Much greater than
        her pride
And perseverance;
A failure
    the concealment of which
Can easily crash
        her integrity;
Can negate the truth of her competence;
Can force her to despise herself
As a lousy liar,
    a hateful hypocrite.

It was,
    perhaps,
Only by confessing to someone
The fact of her failure

In the mission in motherhood,
That she could regain
Her will to live
              and her faith in love.

But to whom could she turn
For a confession that demanded
A pure divine understanding
To keep
        the universe of her soul
                  in place?

iii

The door,
        as usual,
                was opened
By no one but her *"Grand Friend,"*
An old man,
Frail in body,
        but strong in will,
His awe-inspiring head
Sparsely covered
                with snow-white hair,
His wrinkled warm face,
With two soul-seeing black eyes,
Lit by the mystical rays
Of a loving,
        resigned
              smile.

The old man,
Standing on the threshold,

And,
> as usual,
>> expecting his daughter,
His *"Great Young Friend,"*
To rush to him for a vigorous handshake,
But what he saw
>> was
Disturbingly unexpected:
Silent and sad,
> she was standing there,
Her hands,
> left hanging by her sides,
Her tired eyes
> reflecting
The anguish of a tormented soul,
Helplessly
> staring
Into his thoughtful eyes,
As if in any moment
> a fatal quake
Was going to devour away the earth
From under her feet.

Now,
Feeling that he had no time
> to waste
On wondering
> and pondering,
The father,
The old grand friend,
stretched out his hands,
> like wings,
Stepped into the air,
And took the daughter,
> the great young friend,
Tightly into his arms
And said aloud

                in a new voice:
"Cry, cry,
       my friend,
              my daughter!
Tell me,
     tell me,
Where is your son,
                your lovely son?"

iv

After a humbling confession
Of her failure in motherhood,
And admitting her deep ignorance
When it comes to some
                mysterious aspects of life,
She felt that,
       ironically,
              she had saved
The grace of being true to herself;

Now,
     she wiped away her tears
With her expressive fingers,
And her eyes began to shine
With a serene and soft smile,
And her face regained its composure.

And then she closed her eyes
And opened her heart
To the music of her father's words
Falling in a cascade of light
From the top of the gray experience
Down the green gorge of the moment:

"The meaning of life?
No, my dear,
My Love-of-truth,
My precious Honesty!
To think of Life as something
With a general meaning
For everyone,
            everywhere
                      and all times
Is a mere illusive mistake.

The young want to know
A reason,
      a purpose,
           a meaning for life,
And thus they create
A vital need
      for *"Philosophy;"*
Their elders,
      serious as gods,
Think,
   think deep and wide
And,
   eventually,
      think up
Different,
   detailed,
      amazing answers
And become great *"Philosophers."*

The old,
   having passed these two stages,
Spend their remaining time,
As it comes,
Day to day,

       hour to hour,
In remembering the thoughts
                      and ideas,
The doubts and certainties,
The visions and revelations,
                    they had in the past,
But now,
Many of them
Invalidated by time and experience."

At the end of the last sentence
He fell silent,
      and
Looking into the listening eyes of his daughter,
He smiled,
As if waiting for a response.

V

Now,
    the daughter,
To her father
             his *Love-of-Truth*
And his *Precious Honesty,*
Gently rose up to her feet,
Gently bent forward,
And gently kissed his forehead
As a revering response of appreciation.

And the father
Threw his arms around her neck
And kissed the top of her head
                     and said:
"Now the time is ripe for … "

And the daughter
Did not let him finish his sentence,
And said:
" ... for me to get up
And brew a good pot of tea!"

And the father said:
"Then,
   first let me finish
       my boring answer
To my sane and sound grandson."

And the daughter said:
"Yes,
And to your ignorant
      and confused daughter,
          as well!"

And they both burst
      into hearty,
         happy laughter.

vi

"My very dear
   very young friend,
My precious grandson,
Something
That like a single link in a chain,
Begins its existence
From the end of

                its previous identical double,
And its own end comes
                    at the beginning
                              of the next one,
Cannot have any meaning
                    in itself!
And if it remains satisfied
With the mere state
                of its being in the chain,
Well,
Who knows why should the chain
                              be there at all!
And why should we care anyway!
For us,
From the first day
            of our self-awareness
To our last day
When
      whatever we had thought we were,
Including
        the Crown of the Creation,
The Likeness of God,
En-souled with His own holy breath,
Is to be absorbed and lost forever
In the living womb of the earth.

In the blind eye of Nature,
                    my dear grandson,
The life of an *'elephant,'*
                    or of a *'fly,'*
Must have the same meaning
That the life of a *'human being'* can have:"
A single link
        in a meaningless chain.

A heart,
       my dear,
               is a heart,
– The heart of a fly,
              or that of an elephant –
And it is a heart
         while it is beating;
Beating for whom?
Knowingly for the organism,
                 as a whole:
The Elephant,
       the Fly,
             and the Man?
Or as an essentially mechanical function
For its own survival?
No, dear,
       the question is absurd,
And so is,
       perhaps,
             the answer!

Let us think
       that the act of beating
Is the only meaning
             a heart can have,
And let us drink tea together,
             and rejoice!

Then,
    we can either say:
Life has no clear meaning,
Or say that the meaning of life,
At any common moment of our time,
Is whatever we do,
       Right or wrong,

With sadness
> or with delight,
To give a human substance and purpose
To the illusion
> of the passage
>> of that moment
>>> of our time.

Therefore,
> my dear grandson,
That moment in which
> you asked your mother
About the meaning of life:
You were giving
> a human meaning
To the life of the moment
With your state of mind
> and the eternal question.

Time,
> Tea,
>> and Togetherness:
Let us rejoice,
> my dear daughter."

We, Our, and Ours

You are walking with him
in a garden of flowers
in full bloom
          with soft brilliance,
and generously rich
          in diversity.

They,
    the flowers,
        the earthly *houris*,
have captivated you
with the mystical art
        of their shapes and patterns;
with the magical music
        of their shades of colours;
with the sweet words
        of their entrancing scents;
with the divine beauty
        of their miraculous presence.

At this time,
    that is *"the-time-being,"*
you have closed
      the door of perception
to all the things of the past,
and have the feeling of a pilgrim
in the living temple of the Sun.

At this time
you need to be alone;
to be a free and silent *"self,"*
out of the reach of illusions;
but you ought to remember
that you are with an *"other,"*
and you hear him telling,
               with dubious enthusiasm,
the tale of his young,
                  beautiful
                          sister-in-law
who has fallen for a wrong man,
                          disappointing him
by not listening
          to his brotherly advices!
"What makes me shudder with fear,"
                           he says
"is that her reckless choice
May ruin her precious life!"

At this time,
your companion-in-walking
grabs your sleeve
               to stop you,
because,
     all of a sudden,
his eyes,
       passing by a flower bed,
with a peculiar arrangement,
have seen something
                so fascinating
that you must see it
and enjoy the coincidence
                of meaning and absurd:

"Look there,
        it is amazing!
Three patches of flowers,
in the shape of a clover-leaf,
but in three plain colours:
We are looking at our national flag!
Salute!"

At this time
you stand one step back from "We,"
from all your Companions-in-walking,
and then,
from a distance of about
        two-hundred thousand years,
you smile and say: "Salute!"

We,
   and
      Our Nation,
and *Our National Flag!*

Yes,
    We, with our *Ours:*
Our Tribe!
Our People!
Our Nation!
Our Village!
Our Country!
Our Empire!
Our Chieftain!
Our Ruler!
Our King!
Our Emperor,
Our President!

Our Medicine man!
Our Magician!
Our Prophet!
Our Traditions!
Our God Almighty,
    the Beneficent,
    the Avenger,
    the Giver of Honour,
    the Compeller,
    the Giver of Dishonour,
    the Merciful,
    the God!
We,
  Our,
    Ours!

21 December 2014

Mahmud Kianush

Nothing Is Eternal
To be recited at my departure

i

Some people,
        in their seventies,
and many more in their eighties,
when,
        in a peaceful spring,
or in an invigorating summer,
they look at the blue sky
of a beatific,
        entrancing
                sunny day,
they utter a tormented sigh
of sorrow and despair,
because they feel
        they are the victims
of a tyrannical design;
they find themselves merely made
of a handful of dust
        and a bucketful of water
to be used
        as living devices
to test the desirability of life
as a transient,
        sweet,
                beautiful illusion.

Their pain must be so great
that no deity of any religion,
in human form,
        with human soul,
can deeply suffer

and yet
>	remain unchanged.
Once,
>	when I was the age of their sons,
one of them,
in the depth of his agony
in his last converse with me,
as always careful not to be heard
>	>	by the mob,
whispered into my ear,
>	>	saying:
"I hate this Absurd Tyranny,
and for it
I hate,
>	I curse the Mystery!
Now the clay vessel is shattering
>	>	at last,
and all the wine
>	of eighty years,
made by me,
drop by drop,
>	moment by moment,
as my soul,
>	my mind,
>	>	my very own self;
all my wine
made with my visionary
>	>	awareness of history,
with the beauty of my thoughts,
of my ideals,
>	my words,
>	>	my meanings,
and the infinite universe of my heart,
will all be wasted,
>	annihilated,
>	>	forever.

Oh,
    how I hate to be created
by the will
        and the purpose
of some other one,
            whosoever It be!
Oh,
    I hate,
        I hate and curse the Mystery!"

ii

But there are some other people,
who have always been the majority
in every population,
            anywhere on Earth,
every one of whom is born
            with a certain destiny
the book of which is revealed to them,
page by page,
        one page a day only,
from the moment they wake up,
with or without dreams,
           in the morning,
until sleep comes
and puts them into unconscious rest
           at night.

They have their divine faith.
They never fall in doubt
        about anything.
Everything in their world
        is just the way
           it should be;

So their minds and souls are free
from impious,
        futile
                questions.

If they are poor,
and all their time is spent
in a perpetual struggle
                to survive,
they know that the Omniscient knows it all,
and with an innocent sigh
                they silently say:

"Thy will is our contentment!"
Because they are told
                by their holy ancients:
"He exalteth whomsoever He pleaseth,
and He abaseth whomsoever He pleaseth!"
And then,
        of course,
when they happen to see a glimpse
                of the luxurious life
the richest among the rich are living,
they do not fail to reproach their eyes
for looking with envy
                at the worldly wealth,
and their hearts for beating
                with the unfaithful desires,
reminding them of the divine order of things,
by reciting to them
                this ancient holy verse:
"He giveth sustenance
to whom he pleaseth without measure!"

The richest among the rich
who half-heartedly believe in anything
whenever something proves
to be highly profitable
                      in their business of life,
both, in this and in the other world,
wholeheartedly thank
                      the good Almighty One
who has chosen them and loves them
                      as His favourites;
but they live unaware of the fact
that the poorest among the poor
receive the Angel of Death
with a smile of relief and joy,
hearing the cherubim singing in Heaven:
"Hearken to the good tidings
O you who are the poor
                      in the kingdom of earth,
the Kingdom of heaven will be yours!
And always remember,
with your unshakable faith,
                      that
it is easier for a camel to go through
the eye of a needle
                      than for someone
who is rich to enter the Kingdom of Heaven!"

iii

Among the faithless sceptics
who hate and curse
the Mystery of existence
                      and of life,
and the faithful,

>both poor,
who wholeheartedly,
>>and rich,
who half-heartedly,
>>believe
in the fulfilment
>>of the promises
of their good Almighty One,
made through the holy ancients,
regarding the freehold ownership
of a fully-furnished,
>>luxurious villa
in the Kingdom of Heaven,
there must be a very small minority
who have never categorized themselves
>>>under any title,
but by others
they are called by many unpopular names,
names such as
>*"agnostics,"*
>>*"sceptics,"*
>>>*"unbelievers,"*

Or even,
>in the eyes of the zealots,
>>shameless *"infidels."*

and only a few of the deists,
sometimes,
>with some due respect,
think him to be a *"freethinker,"*
without receiving his thoughts into their hearts.

These
       (let us call them *"heretics,"*
Or *"I-don't-know-ists"*
              without asking their consent)
These *"Idontknowists"*
do not want to know
             when and how
the Universe and Life on Earth began,
and by whose will and purpose.

               * * *

They think
that no one has ever been able
to decipher the secret
of the Great Mystery,
not ever since a pair of animals,
             male and female
somewhere
      in a jungle
became aware of their nakedness
and felt ashamed
        and lost
            and abandoned
and left the world of the wild
             with fear and fury,
until now
that they have become too *fruitful*
and *have replenished the earth*
          in a mad way,
and *have subdued it*
       to the edge of its destruction
with a chaotic army
of seven-thousand-million
           mutinous personnel.

               * * *

They think
that everything in the universe,
or, in another word,
the universe as one whole entity
is always in motion
      and changing,

and only
the never-changing law of change
       is eternal.

        * * *

They think
that only those who want to believe
in the existence of two worlds,
one temporal
    for the body with soul,
and the other eternal
      for the soul without body,
are the forces of destruction,
      without willing,
and the enemies of life on earth,
       without knowing,
and the worshippers of death
       with awe and hate,
their minds are museums of horror
with images of tombs and worms,
of skulls and bones,
of the damned souls,
of the hellish demons,
of scenes of punishment by fire,
fire, fire, flaming fire,
bodies burning,
eyes,
 and hearts,
    and hands burning,

mouths,
> and ears,
>> and tongues burning,
pain, pain, pain,
> cries of pain,
all in anticipation of what?
of the eternal life in the gardens of heaven.

> * * *

They think
that all those children of Adams and Eves
who have sound brains,
uninfected with the syphilis
of the ancestral unreasoned *ideas,*
> and superstitious *beliefs,*
>> and miraculous *expectations,*
>>> and answered *prayers:*
deeply,
> sincerely,
>> uncompromisingly hate
to be regarded
> as the identical members of a herd,
or to be patronised by someone
> of their own species
as their *shepherd,*
> their *saviour,*
>> their *leader,*
>>> their earthly *representative,*
>>>> their divine *interceder,*
because they think
that there are two realities:
one the *Reality of the World,*
> in the World,
>> for the World,

and the other,
the *Reality in Man*
     by Man,
       for Man,
but our life on Earth,
out of the Eden of the Wild,
      began
when we taught ourselves,
by love and experience,
how to change
    the irrational,
     enigmatic,
      callous reality of the World
into the meaningful,
   righteous,
     amusing,
      imaginative reality of Man.

       * * *

They think
that by creating an inner world
      for ourselves
we have become
the outside observers of the universe,
a universe in which
    no one,
     nothing,
      can be aware
of what we are in our individual selves;
and, therefore,
all the characters of our divine myths
have their familiar existences
     only in our inner world,

and by worshipping them
we worship our creative imagination,
we call to our help
our known human god,
not the god unknown
                as the mystery of all mysteries.

iv

It is said that
only the never-changing law of change
                          is eternal.
It is the same if we say:
"Nothing is Eternal!"

But I,
as one of the believers of this creed,
also believe
that whatever is the status of things
between the beginning
and the end of one stage of change,
is eternal in itself.

Once,
      in a bright night,
in a sky full of shining stars,
suddenly I found myself
                talking to a faint star,
now appearing, now disappearing:

"O, the farthest star
In the blue dome,
What did you mean

When you said: "Stranger!
I am your eyes
And you are the light of my heart;
In this night of primeval darkness
A friend sends you greetings."

It was not a game
               of self-deception;
I was not talking to myself;
it seemed to me
that at the same moment
the Mystery
               was also looking at me
through the eye of that star,
and listening to me
through the ear
               of silence
                           of Infinity.

Being so close to the Mystery of Mysteries
in a moment of cosmic ecstasy,
that blissful rare moment
becomes eternity:
Oh!

Yes,
I as one of the adherents of
               "Nothing-is-eternalism,"
having recently entered
the eighty-first year of my life,
on my way to hospital,
while waiting for the red light
               to change,
through the window of the ambulance

among the impatient pedestrians
I caught sight of a young woman
whose big bulging belly,
and the expression on her face,
were showing her to be
in the last few days of her pregnancy.

I put my hand
on my fast and irregular
                beating heart,
and with a mysterious smile,
said in my voiceless mind

"my tired heart,
thank you so much
for your three billion beats of life.
I don't expect you to know
that nothing is eternal,
not the earth,
nor the sun,
nor the universe,
but I know that soon
you will retire and rest,
and surely you will have
your complete share of
                the human eternity.
Your relief,
as fresh and strong
                as you were eighty years ago,
has already begun
                passionately beating
in the wombs of all the young,
                pregnant women
who are waiting for the traffic lights to change,
to cross the street of habits,

to join their men
in the roofed oases of pleasure and pain,
at the clamorous coasts of wonderment.
Let there be
    no questions,
        no complaints!
It was
    and it will be
        what it is!"

To Lila

I thought of you
in the halo of a white smile.

Unaware of my sudden presence,
you were standing upright,
looking into the space
                       at something
far beyond the sun's
                       field of vision.

At just that moment
a tree of light soared up
in the dark space
                       of my unconscious self;
a fresh,
        strong
                image
in an unheard poem;
a full bloomed red rose
                       floating
on the pearly white pond of the full moon
in the clear sky of a mythical night;
a green,
        melodic dream
                       of a goddess,
resistant to all earthly,
                realistic,
                          interpretations.

It all was so strange
that it made me sink
     into a frozen silence.
How could she know
     that I was going to tell her
about making a poem
     in her magnificent image?

Before I could give voice to one word
of my unwanted statement,
     she said,
without turning to face me:
"Hearken,
  o, you,
    poet,
The poem is I myself;
Try,
  if you care,
    to read me
in solemn silence."

18 March 2015

Genesis III
For Giles Goodland

The sky was thoroughly clouded
and the window panes
                        deeply blurred,
when,
      first,
            from a distance,
I looked at my image
reflected in the mirror
                  on the mantelpiece.

I felt I had no reason
                  not to be content
with my image
as seen in the eyes of the world,
and so
I continued to enjoy
              watching it
with a noble smile.

But soon there came a time
when the transitory clouds
                broke up
                    and vanished,
and the unaffected sun
              re-appeared
in her full
        enlightening
              radiance,
and the clear sight
              returned to the window panes:

I stepped,
        as if in a mystic trance,
close
      close to the mirror
                on the mantelpiece,
and was shocked and deranged
                      by what I saw!

Only a glimpse of what I saw
was far more horrible
than my lifetime experience
      of nightmares and fears,
          of disgust and nausea,
              of contempt and shame,
and I heard a loud and painful cry,
calling:
    "Oh, God!"

28 April 2015

Mahmud Kianush

Blessed Are the Wolves

Who art Thou?
Only Thou mayest know,
                no one else!

The wolves are perfect
                and sincere
                        in what they are;
and what they are
is what Thou wantedest them to be.

Yes,
    I know:
Their state of existence is,
                in essence,
                        almost,
the same as those of Thy other living things:
a struggle for survival,
with,
    perhaps,
            only one goal:
passing their selfish genes
to their next generations,
                with glorious success,
and they themselves
having to be vanished
                into thy eternal mystery.

The wolves,
like all the rest of Thy living things,
have never been,
            for a good and proper life,

in need of any guidance
through a fellow species
                         appointed by Thee
as Thy messenger,
to propagate the words of Thy mouth.

What is wrong with us human beings,
proud of being created in Thy likeness,
Oh Thou,
        who remainest unknown forever?

1 May 2015

Suddenly

Suddenly
the visualisation of history
became easy for my mind,
just like saying "No,"
after breaking the nightmare,
in answer to someone
who has always heard "Yes."

It so happened
                that Existence,
with all its confusions,
from the beginning of the history
until the moment
                when
my form is also disintegrated,
simplified itself for me
into the shape and the meaning
                of a simple event,
like putting a boundless ocean
                into its small name
which is only two drops of sound.

Suddenly a bird
            came from nowhere,
and perched on the ground,
                near me,
but too unaware of,
            or too unconcerned
                with my presence,
and began to peck the loving earth
with hungry appetite,
            but in a wary state.

When it picked up and swallowed
its first bit of some edible thing,
it began to glance around
                        with apprehension.

Nothing had happened,
nor had I given any assertive force
                        to my presence:
Yet the bird,
in a sudden change of mood,
seemingly felt seeing
in its inner world of instincts
a fatal storm of calamity
                    rising,
and began to raise a turmoil
with its wings and cries,
and arrowed itself
                into the infinite space
like a cry of torture,
and disappeared
            in the void of nowhere.

Can it be explained
Any briefer,
        or simpler
                    than that?
Let us leave it
            and go.

1988

Amusement

All around me
there spreads a desert
        to beyond the horizons
                in deep silence:
the eyes of the space
        darkened and disturbed
by the bitter memories
from the vertiginous,
        repetitious tales.

But,
– like some quivering smiles
of a star at night
which breaks,
with her intimacy and sorrow,
the abysmal void of darkness –
for me
at the farthest expanses of perception,
the flight of two doves
comes to sight with grace
in a golden mist,
        near the moon.

This is an amusement
which still,
        now and then,
opens out a sure way,
from the solitude of my heart
into the infinite domain of awareness.

1986

Now in Silence

Now,
within the darkness
 of the silence in my head
suddenly,
 a cry explodes,
and breaks,
 breaks,
 and shatters
the infernal tedium,
and scatters it in powder
into my space view
 all around.

Now,
I have an explosion
 in my inner self,
a strange explosion
that fails to break down to the ground
all the soaring heights
with fire and blood;
that fails to raise the ashes
 of Love and Man
up to the summit of the firmament.

1976

These Stars

In order that the stars,
those silent watchers
who twinkle at us
             from too far a distance,
begin to speak with us,
we flew many kites of paper
                 and of lunacy.

We gave
       to a number of them
some beguiling names,
and as is the way
             with the wishful thinkers,
called them
and asked for their deliverance,
sometimes
through a song
          of soft and sweet words,
and sometimes
with the volcanic emotion
                of a biting prayer.

But it so seems
that all our efforts
                are futile,
and that amongst all of those stars
there is not even one
which,
      with love or hate,
watches over us,
            or is aware
of our existence

                    and our afflictions;
and worse than all,
even if the earth
                    would eventually burn
by our anger
in the fire of our despair,
it will have no effect
                    in any one of them.

1985

Perhaps the Earth

O you,
       who are standing there,
with your eyes wide open,
waiting for the Unknown to come,
you
    who have always lost
the great chance
of bursting into bloom,
perhaps the Earth,
early in the morning,
had emptied everything
                        she had in her lap
into the hands of the wind.

1971

It is Only the Wind

It is the wind,
        forceful and wild,
and it has been a long time
              since it began
galloping around,
            like a giant swordsman,
slashing the air,
        disturbing the peace of space:

O you,
     my old friend,
now standing there
            like a stranger,
your mouth locked with fear,
your water-like eyes
fixed onto the dust of the road,
with your treasure of love
              almost lost,
and tired of the sufferings endured
on account of affections,
yet do not forget that
           it is only "wind,"
and can do nothing but hurting
the peaceful,
      pure hearts
with darkening dust.

Yes,
    whatever it is,
and whatever it does,
it is only "Wind",
         not the conquering "Sword!"

Then,
>   for God of Love's sake,
in absence of the voiced word of "Hello,"
– suppressed by fear –
give us a friendly message
with the look of your eyes.

No matter how wild it is,
or how forceful,
yet it is only "Wind,"
with all is wild force
it can only take our "Voice" away.

We Are Going Far Away

We try to forget
so that our eyes can see
                with our love,
so that our ears can hear
                with freedom
the music of the moments
without any regret for the past …

Where are you,
          O, the wretched?
Now your ear-rending roars of pride
cannot act as a cloud of dust
to blur the view of our road to freedom.

We are going far away
                from you,
but not like dogs,
previously conditioned
to the meanings of certain smell;
we are going away
from the shade of the first
                primordial Tree,
in companionship with Water
to the threshold of the Sun;
and will never turn our heads
to look back for a moment
lest it would give the impression
that we are taking you along with us.

Mahmud Kianush

This is the morning
              of the first primordial day,
and we leave behind
              and forget
a night in which
the most horrible nightmare
                    separated us
from whatever you were,
from whatever you did,
from whatever you saw.

1973

And This Blind Rat

We have not hidden Love
in the labyrinthine tunnels
                      of our skulls;
nor have we secretly entertained her
in the sacred,
        safe,
                seclusion of our hearts.

The blind rat's search
through the tunnels of his anger and fun
with tens of thousands kinds of lamps,
is all in vain

With his teeth biting deep
into his devouring greed,
beyond the numbers are the heads
                          he has broken,
beyond the number the hearts
                          he has torn apart,
but he still has not found
                      what he thinks
he has lost in us.

If only he could have ever heard
the angels of truth
                who ardently say:
"Man in the sunshine
                  is the shadow of Love;
without its shadow,
            Love will not die.

She will live on
in the green imagination of God,
without any apprehension
from the death of shadow.

Reposeful roams about Love,
reposeful and relaxed.

Market of the Day

Here is the Market of the Day,
in the centre of the town,
with its great seasonal sale of Desires.

Come with your stories:
With the anxieties of days;
and the sorrows of nights;
With all that which is called
achievement of a life time;
Come with your melancholies of nights!
We sell Desires,
in all desirable forms and colours,
                              at half price.

"How much are
            these red velvet curtains, sir?"

I admire your taste!
These curtains,
            in any room,
with their glittering crimson colour,
give a new appearance to everything,
making them
            much, much more
eye-catching and precious.

"About the durability of their fabric
and the fastness of their colour,
I want to know the truth!"

About their colour
you mustn't worry at all:
It is natural and pure,
                      fadeless and fast:
Blood of the youth,
from the East and the West,
processed
          and produced
by steel and gunpowder.
And about their durability,
                      I assure you
that they are the miracle
of the century's technology par excellence:
Their warps made of the endurance
of all the victims of hunger,
and their woofs made of the ignorance
of all the victims of servitude!
if you would care to accept
my word of honour, Sire,
I assure you
that the colour
          and durability
of our curtains of the day
are much,
      much,
              more than perfect.

It is the great seasonal sale of Desires!
Come with your tales
                  and your sorrows;
We sell Desires,
in all desirable forms and colours,
all at half price.

1967

No Pretensions

Now,
it is not a time for pretensions,
because we have fought against nature
effectively
           and more than our needs demand.

On whose side has been the victory?
Ask this
           from the clouds and the wind,
from the sun
           and the earthquakes,
and from Death
           also.

In this time of ours,
when both,
           the divinely sent,
and the self-appointed,
           messengers
now and then
come back,
           tired and sad
to repeat their old lulling tales,
with some new tones and styles
into the receptive,
           easily-lured ears,
it is us
who are standing up
           against ourselves.

All the things so far said,
All the things so far done
And the things that remain
                        to be said and done
cannot hide us
from our weakness and ignorance
under the shadow of our illusions.

If we are ashamed,
what is the cause of our shame?
If our heart is full of resentment,
or our throat is choking with anger,
who has made us resent with anger?

Nothing is left in our memory
but the zealous habit of hiding
the unhealable wound
                        of this shame,
and the damnable deepening
of this resentment
                        in our heart,
and the mindless keeping of this anger
in perpetual broiling
                        in our throat.

What and all
                we have had
and have brought with us
                        as our possessions
since the occurrence
                        of the Great Mishap,
or the Unruly Event,
or whatever any everyman
of anywhere

    would like to call them,
are nothing
   but
the different nonsensical versions
of one and the same story:
that is our battle
against our own shadows
in the sphere of a mysterious spell
which might be not a spell at all.

Though there is here an arena,
and a vast one too,
open from all sides,
spread to beyond
     the borders
of stupidity and remorse,
we are not obliged
     to perform
any competition,
    anyhow.

For how long can we let ourselves
      be flattered
by smiling sweetly
at the face of the mirror?
or by hearing our own sweet bravos
on their return from the mountains?

Now,
it is not a time for pretensions;
let us pause and ponder
     for a short while,
because the Sun
will not turn black

with the smoke of
                our sighs of sorrows,
and the Earth
will not be thrown
                out of its orbit
by our moaning cries of complaints,
but our blackened heart
that has been beating
                too long
in a broken rhythm
                and out of its orbit,
Will eventually end in madness.

From our dreams of dread
                in caves
to our exulting flight to the Moon;
from the hanging gardens of Babylon
to the gas chambers of Auschwitz:
we have committed
too many acts of insipid,
                foul
                    madness.

This is the bitter cry of despair,
and I have heard it from many mouths:
From Omar Khayyam,
in his rose gardens
                of skulls and bones;
and from Jean-Paul Sartre,
in his nauseous tales of angst
                and the absurd.
But all these messengers of doubts
                and despairs,
in order to disturb the peace
                of my mind

implicitly wanted me
to have a mind
            well collected
                      and keen.
Now that I am blissfully anguished
with purity of pain,
I scatter the red shouts of madness
on the wide roads of the wind.

Stop the game of colours and forms:
My concept of it all,
the simple,
          free-of-all-pains glory,
does not give itself
              to any form,
                      any face:
Either Love,
      in her passage through me
becomes a dance,
           a song,
                 a tale;
or I,
    in my passage through life,
like the wind,
        in its passage
                  across the sea,
I see my image in her waving mirror.

We are coming from
               the shadow of dust,
we smile in the light of rain:
One leaf,
through the lust of the breeze,
talks to another leaf,
and we take the occurrence

as our own story;
but when the breeze lies down
the narration of the story
                    discontinues
all abruptly,
            unexpectedly,
                        by sheer accidence,
and then
another season begins
                its course
just from the end of our unfinishedness.
And the lust of the breeze
whose sleep in the cradle of wakefulness
turns to a sweet trance
by our lullabies,
keeps its ever-fresh
                never-tiring eyelids
wide open.
Now
it is not a time for pretensions.
In this blessed
            pure chance
let us eat,
        drink,
                and laugh:
Haah, haah!
In this great show of magic
a word of incantation,
a cloud of smoke,
a serene dance
a sweet song:
and
    finito!

1972

Now See It As ...

Now see it as cherry blossoms
in the sunshine
of an azure blue sky,
but in the snow garden
of a callous winter.

Now hear it as the exhilarating song
of a strange bird,
hidden inside the foliage
                    of some trees,
not far from where you are standing,
in a friendly forest,
                    free from the fear
of the ferocious prowling predators,
and its spring air,
                    fresh and pure,
throbbing with the sweet scents
                        of herbs and flowers.

But just at the moment
                    when you,
absorbed in the bliss
of the enrapturing melody of the bird,
are trying to hold
on to the silent stillness of perception,
the strange bird stops singing.

You wait,
and your still silence waits,
and waiting waits longer than long,
so,
    at the long last,

waiting proves to be in vain:
Now the day is nearing its end,
and the darkness has begun murmuring
into the eyes of the light:

Now the strange bird
                has taken away
everything that mattered to you
in connection with the Event:
its own dominating,
                but invisible presence,
its exhilarating,
                enrapturing song,
and with them
                all the directions
of any rewarding search.

Now you are left,
                alone and tired,
with the mystery
of the strange bird
inside the darkening shell
                of your memory,
in the autumnal air
of the friendly forest,
                warm and sweet,
throbbing with the pulses
of scents and colours
of dreaming fruits
                and flying leaves.

Now I see it as a ripened poem
and the awakening taste
                of an old poet.

8 July 2015

Oath

Now again you!
Here you are again!
You,
      the people,
and for you a sweet song
with the unpleasant voice
                      of a blind man
in his dark,
      sickening seclusion
from the bright summit of insight.

Today,
      I went
to the burning spring of the Sun,
with all the sincerity of my hatred,
more naked than
              the spirit of the winter,
and in its bitter ancient waters
washed away
          the filth of disbelief,
the thick layer of which
was going to burst my skin
in its heavy grip,
heavier than the grip of cognition.

Now that I have performed
                    my ablutions,
I take an oath
        and swear
by the purity of Amnon's blooming
in the sunshine of Tamar's hatred,

I swear by the sacredness of the swine,
I swear that there has never,
                        never,
never been anything in my heart
but the Love of Life,
Love of Humanity.

1967

Evening of Togetherness

It was a quiet night,
and the weather in a mood
neither exciting,
                nor irritating:
A soft drizzling rain,
in the absence of my awareness,
was taking me out of the present.

Behind me was a wall,
following me,
more importunate,
                more insolent,
than my own shadow,
separating me
from the sphere of voices
                and windows.
I was walking,
        saying to myself:
"To Where?"
And the question echoed in my head:
"toooo wheeeeeere!"

Suddenly I realized
that the voice
        was not mine:
I stopped
    and my eyes
filled with the light of your eyes,
a light that seemed to be exuding
the entrancing waft of
        a mysterious opium.

And your voice,
with the same resonance of sorrow
flowing from the orbits
of all the wanderers,
                        repeated:
"To where,
      well,
            to where?"

And then you said again:
"Aloneness,
      rain,
            and a night
in which every voice
                is a wall,
and the light of every window
a flaming sword,
            turning every way
to prevent you from picking the apple,
to deprive you of tasting friendship,
through the miracle
of the first divine sin."

And then,
you stood silent for a moment,
and the look of your eyes
gave a bitter smile
and you said to me:
"Well,
    now let us go!"

1967

Anyhow

Anyhow,
in the boundless,
              hanging cave,
lonelier than Silence,
more silent than
              the absolute Remorse,
he rose up.

The flaming sun
with the true hell of
              bitter thoughts,
in the body of a teardrop
fell down
on the thirsty salt desert
              of his hand,
and the night
flooded into the goblet
of his bleak expectations.

And then,
in the boundless,
              hanging cave,
lonelier than Silence,
more silent than
              the absolute Remorse,
he sat down.

1961

Mahmud Kianush

Thou Art Thine Own Cosmos
For Joanne Arnott & Giles Goodland

When Time was still untouched
By the curse of History,
And passed away unwatched,
Counted only by days and nights;
When I had begun seeing things
In the sounds of their names,
And could evidently see
That seeing was not believing;
When looking at one's father
With doubt and dislike
Was not yet considered
An insolent act of irreverence;
I could clearly see,
With my inner eyes,
That in everything whatsoever
Something was missing.

|

And ever since then,
Ceaselessly,
        tirelessly,
                I have been

In search of those missing *"Somethings"*
In my thoughts and my dreams,
In the light of hope,
And in the dark of despair,
In the songs of the loving birds,

And the in words of the wise souls,
Across the wordless sounds of the Universe,
Before the eyes of its blind Galaxies.

|

And
    now
        that
I have brought my search
To a personal,
    Reserved
        end,
With this intuitive belief
That I have found
My own missing *"Something,"*
I would like to leave a friendly note
For those fellow searchers
Who happen to be
Intuitively familiar
With the alphabet of my silence.

|

At long last
I decided to think
That my unique Garden of Eden,
[The lost paradise of every wonderer],
Was nothing but the unique Womb
Of my unique Mother,
Situated between two branching rivers:

One the arterial,
                named *Gihon*,
And the other,
            the venous,
                    named *Pishon*;
With two trees in the centre of the Garden:
One deciduous,
                with red sweet blossoms,
And the other evergreen,
                      with green bitter leaves.

      |

After being banished from the Garden,
I was left lost and alone,
Wandering,
        in oblivion of my past,
Surrounded by myriads of mysterious things,
In whose appearances,
By now familiar to my tired eyes,
And not dismaying anymore,
Still they seemed to have something
                              missing,

Something that may make them
                        real
In what they seem they are.

      |

Now,
Having found those missing *"Somethings"*
In my Personal Universe,

As the sweet harvest of my Personal Search
In the wilderness of *thorns* and *thistles,*
I keep them to myself,
                        for myself;
But,
As a farewell to my fellow-wanderers,
I care to say that:
                "The Genesis,
The Garden of Eden,
The Doubting and Rebellion,
The Odyssey of Restlessness,
And the Homecoming,
Are all
      solely,
           only
                and exclusively
Private and Personal."

|

I am my own Cosmos.

Mahmud Kianush

Perhaps ...
For a friend-in-poetry
David Pendlebury

I have walked on Earth
for hundreds of thousands of years
as the sole observer of Things and Others.
I have walked alone,
forced by an inner necessity
to create all and everything anew,
watching them in amazement,
in a state of near lostness,
but not with dread and despair.

Perhaps,
all this time,
I had been talking,
with my Inner Voice,
to the feeling of a Void,
as boundless as the whole Universe.

Perhaps
it has always been,
not the Void of anything,
but only the Self of my Other I,
always real,
            always present,
always listening to my Inner Voice.

Perhaps,
        now,
            at last,
the time has come for me
to stop my Cosmological Quest
                        and rest
as a wandering dreamer

returning home,
>
> awe-stricken,
>
> > heavy-hearted,
> >
> > > empty-handed,

but yet fully satisfied,
from his long divine journey
across the timeless history of a universe,
acting like an entity of hands,
devoid of mind,
>
> devoid of heart.

Perhaps, now,
at the beginning of the Big Rest,
the Silence of the Universe
is merely the echo
of my Big,
>
> Unbanged,
>
> > Bitter
> >
> > > Laughter.

16 January 2017

Mahmud Kianush

The Blossom of Astonishment

i

I have not ascended,
nor have I descended;
scattered I am,
and boundless.

I have nothing in my memory,
nor have I forgotten anything;
out of the domain of Time,
with no past,
          no future.

On the border of Yes and No,
in the distance between
          Being and Nothingness,
between Reality and Illusion,
I am tasting my thoughts,
I am drinking my thoughts,
I am silently shouting out my thoughts,
I am freeing my thoughts
from the prison of bone, blood, and flesh.

I kiss the Sun,
I greet the Plants,
I embrace the Water with fervour,
and sing my newest song
          into the ear of Stone.

For paper,
Let me have the wings of the butterflies
living in the Valley of Sorrows;
for pen,
let me have the quills of the angels
from the kingdom of Lucifer,
and for ink,
let me have the pure blood of all the girls
who died before puberty,
how else can I let be known
        that
in the infinite sphere of my mind
        has exploded
the star of such a new song
that reshaping it into words
is far beyond
        the power of speech:

A gem is embedded in my heart
the shine and splendour of which
is too dazzling to bear.

A spring of soothing freshness,
welling up in my head,
        rushing on
with the speed of wild tornadoes,
but with the silence of the forbidden thoughts,
drags me along
on the surface of all the rivers around the globe.

A plant grows in my vision,
with the blossoms of eye-pleasing colours
and of sweet scents of freedom,
soaring above the pride of my devotion.

ii

The sun turned to dust,
mountains became deluges of molten stones,
and oceans broke their vow of patience
                                      with roars of fire:
I have come into a gracious unity
with the magical gravity of dreamful sleeps,

with the lightness of angels in their dancing steps,
with the confusion of storms in their thoughts,
        and,
with the peacefulness
                of the oceans of ice.

I retell History
from its foreword to its epilogue,
in a single word.
I chronicle Creation,
from the moment it began as a vision
to the last moment of its complete realisation,
in a smile,
and I cross the infinite sea of death.

iii

Let them know
            that
in the eternity of a moment of bliss,
when our hands were melting into each other
in the sanctuary of primordial unity,
we burned into ashes,
in the bonfire of our drumming hearts,
all the palaces of marble, greed and ruthlessness,
all the thrones of ivory, idiocy and arrogance,

all the curtains of brocade, lewdness and lechery,
all the carpets of silk, silver, gold, hypocrisy and deceit.
On the whole earth,
nowhere a single tree
        has ever been felled;
nowhere a wall of any kind
        has ever been built.
The pure womb of Jungle is still clean
from the deadly semen of gunpowder,
and clean is still the Oysterland in the sea
from the stupid pulse of searching,
        plucking hands,
because I entered naked
into the sunshine of her looks,
and performed my ablution
        in the spring of her smile,
and sowed the seeds of a spontaneous oath
in the well-watered field of my lips.

I am hearing the red corals singing;
I am intoxicated with the wine of stars;
I am feeling the warm caresses
        of the moonlight fingers;
I am swaying between Creating and Being Created.

iv

There is still no absurd image of any name
in the eyes of anything in the world;
the persevering hands of the righteous
have not yet been subdued
by the marching feet of the psychopath;
the seas have not yet been greeted
by the secluded valleys;
the peaceful,

                dreamless sleep of diamonds
have not yet been shattered
by the persistent,
           sinister
                    knockings
of the searching, blind pickaxe;
because she entered naked
into the sunshine of my looks,
and performed her ablution
           in the spring of my smile.

Centuries and centuries
before the invading attacks of Gods
we had been the unrivalled rulers of the whole world.

Centuries and centuries
before the rebellion of Satans
we freed our minds
from the burden
           of pride and egocentrism.

We who have no connections with the Passed-awayers,
and have no messages for the Not-yet-have-comers,
are inscribing the Life History of the Have-passed-awayers
for the Living of the Future
on the rock of our uniting hands.

We see the glowing face of Victory,
with all its glorious adornments,
as reflected in the empty mirror of Defeat
and let our two lives become one
on the borderline between these two illusions.

V

We are human beings;
we are forgetful,
because we have forgotten
        the rebelling blood
of the young dreamers,
shed on the burning sands
        of ancient traditions.

We have forgotten
the hurried tempo of plundering hooves
on the panic-stricken cobblestones,
in the deep sleep of the peaceful towns.

We have forgotten
the devouring crawl of flames
on the bodies of the majestic walls
and royal curtains of Vanity.

We have forgotten
the crucified regrets of the Forsaken,
and the blasphemous trusts of the Mystics
burned at the stake in their ecstasy.

The last beats of the downtrodden hearts,
buried in the solid silence

of the great walls of sweat and blood,
still cry out:
        "Life, Life!"

The sizzling tremors of the burning bodies
in the furnace of the race supremacy
still whisper with some hope
into the stone-deaf ear
of despair:
        "Love, Love!"

The ashes of the fearless thoughts,
chastised for the sin of being visionaries,
thrown in the tempestuous river of bigotry
by the hands of hypocrisy,
ashes that still repeat
              in the loud voices
of waves and winds:
        "Unity, Unity!

And we do not hear outcries
because we are human beings,
and the murmurs of our passions
                    and desires
are much louder and more fluent!

vi

We are human beings;
we are lost in bewildering astonishment:

While we had our hands
stretched out towards heaven,
in adoration of our deities,
we were also crushing
every good thing to dust
under our feet of massacre and pillage,
in our satanic missions of prophetic conquest.

While we were thrusting our sword
into the flesh of the subdued,
            down to their bones,
we were also pulling out
the venomous thorns of sorrow
from the agonized souls
of the distressed and the despaired.

While,
            with our ceaseless efforts,
we were trying to build
our small and poorly huts
on the border of storms and floods,
we were also turning
great cities of art and culture
into barren plains,
or green pastures for a nomadic life.

While we were letting
            our kisses of love
touch the pearl white breasts of our beloveds
as softly as the rays of love
in the eyes of the mating doves,
we were also throwing our chosen brothers,
the most favoured sons of our fathers,
into the deep,
        dry,
            deadly
                cisterns
  of jealousy,
        insecurity,
             and hatred:

Because we were human beings;
Because we are lost in bewildering astonishment.

vii

Let them fly to the near and far planets;
let them build up cities of crystal
      on the bottom of the great seas;
let them extract shining ruby wine
from the barren womb of sand deserts;
let them create a new alloy
    of life,
          stone,
                and fire
in thousands of peaceful towns
by only pushing a weird button!

But if these are what they know
as their wonderful achievements,
let them hear that I know
some simple things
that stand,
in their greatness and glory
far above their universe:
the meetings of Loving Eyes,
the greetings of Sincere Smiles,
because Man is the Blossom of Astonishment
and astonishment yields no other fruit
but futility alone.

viii

O, you,
        the vigorous Spring,
you, the faithful season of the year,
you, the god of the inevitable creations,
hold me,
      like a lost but returned child,

in your fresh and soothing arms,
and wash away the dust
from my cold and pallid face
with the kisses of a new freshness.

You are not forgetful;
you are not lost in astonishment;
you are not human being;
you respect all our offerings,
             no matter what they are,
and you renew your act
             of giving gifts and graces,
                          boons and riches,
in the jubilant festival of leaves
             and blossoms.

O, Season of Affections,
I have not come from a long journey,
but I am exhausted and dust-covered.
I have not lived the Alwaysness,
but I am full of the memories and pains
             of Alwaysness.
I have not been God,
but I began to carry
             the heavy load of History
long before the appearance of gods:

And now,
with my back bent
             to the verge of breaking
under the pressure of this wild weight,
I am trembling to the core of my consciousness.

Now,
like a loving mother,
take me onto your comforting lap,
and let my face be covered
with the soft, fragrant hair
      of your beloved balming breeze.

ix

Tell me,
      O you,
the great men of victory,
the echoes of whose names
have toppled the loftiest of the strong towers,
and the sound of whose footsteps
pierces through steel and granite,
like the wrath of God,
what is more beautiful
than the voiceless words of light
expressed in the meetings of Loving Eyes,
in the eternity of a moment?
What is more victorious
than the revelation of
      a pre-existent acquaintance
at the first exchange of sincere smiles?
What is more glorious
than the pledge of an eternal unity
signed through the exchange of cosmic kisses
from the inner core of the heart?

x

Terror is pounding in the heart of the space,
and Darkness,
      with a barbarian insolence,
has hung its direful nameplate

on the shining forehead of the Sun.
Wines have become blood in their weird taste,
and eyes daggers in their belligerent glares.
Feelings and emotions are gluttonously chewed
as delicious morsels of deceit.
And friendship is a colourful deception;
a mask which keeps the reality concealed.

Come,
           let us stop following them!
Their path is one of deviation!
Let us leave them with their
           calamitous fate;
to the fatal curse of friendlessness!
Two hearts united in Love and Truth,
would never feel alone,
but they are,
and will always remain
           alone in their millions.

Let us get far away from
the dry desert of their delusions and dreads,
and try to find,
through the safe and secure valley of our songs,
the blessed path of purity and light;
and make a bower in the lush garden
           of our conversations,
a bower of the fragrant branches and leaves
of our spontaneous affections,
with a lantern hanging from its ceiling,
a lantern of the stars of undisturbed dreams.

Let us forget the poisonous glittering of gold,
and remain happy with the sun,
because the sun is a coin with one side
and one image,
and we are the adorers of oneness.

xi

Do you hear it?
The crested larks are singing.
They are talking with the Goddess of Spring.
We know their language.
We also always talk
with the spring
              in their language.

I am feeling the fresh fragrance of their songs
on the shores of
              the vast expanses of my body,
and the bliss of a new life
                    is flowing in my blood.

Let us call the crested larks
with their real unspoken name,
and implore them to come
          and perch
on the blooming bush of our adoring eyes.

You love the crested larks;
you love them more than you love me,
because they sing so merrily like you,
and like you,
              free from hopes and fears of future,
gambol on the lush grass in the meadow;
but as for me,
              it is only by looking at you
that I think of the crested larks,
because I love you more than I can love them.

The pleasant cool of the breeze,
like fine drops of wine and milk,
falls on blossoms of your lips,
and on the fresh leaves of your body.

It is delightful to watch
the golden tassels of corns
in the sunshine of a summer day,
but watching you shaking your hair
is more delightful
even in a cold and cloudy morning
               in the winter time.

Two graceful branches
of a unique
            white jasmine
                      in full bloom:
just a faint reminder of your bare arms
stretched out in the blue brilliance
            of the open air.

Climbing up and down a pair of twin hills
covered with sweet scented herbs
and beautiful wild flowers
is no doubt a pleasant and healthy pastime,
but letting my eyes leisurely wander
up and down and around your bare breasts
is a ritual of adoration
            in tracing back
the long precreational thinking
of a perfect shape
            for the love of life.

xii

A lone gazelle jumps down
from the top of a huge rock,
and stands at the edge of a small spring;
it casts a glance at the limpid bubbling water,
and then
           raises his head up
and keeps looking into the space
           above the huge rock
until another gazelle appears
           from behind it:
This is the meaning of Life!
And you know this well,
and we know it well;
but they try to make
           the heart of the Space
pound with terror,
and to hang the direful nameplate of
           Darkness
On the shining forehead of the Sun.

We will never yield to them!
In the face of fatal lifequakes
           we will laugh!
In the grip of deadly deluges of time
           we will sing!
And if we fall and fail to rise again,
with the light and warmth of our blood
will salute the Sun,
will salute the Spring
      and the Wonders of the Green World.

We reject their aims and beliefs;
we get far away from the dry desert
           of their delusions and dreads,
and try to find,
through the safe and secure valley

of our songs,
the blessed path of light,
                    beauty,
                              and truth.

We take a journey
from the Dawn of the Day
            to its Sunset
so that we can have for the Night
a righteous road of return
to the dawn of another day of Life.

xiii

And lo,
on the border of Yes and No,
in the dreamful awareness between
              Being and Nothingness,
between Reality and Illusion,
I live my thoughts,
I taste my thoughts,
I drink my thoughts,
I scatter my thoughts in the shape of words
across the Eternal Infinity of Space
I take my Thoughts out of
              the winter greenhouse of Feelings
and place them
in the warm
              and living sunshine
                            of another Spring.

Original Persian, Tehran – 8 May 1959
English version, London – 16 November 2017
Dedicated to Pari Kianush

Zubaida
Dedicated to all the mothers
of the world of all times.

Zubaida,
the Dandelion,
the loving Goddess of Messages,
                              did not know
that she was bearing in her earthly form
the pure spirit of her mother,
                              Eve,
and in her eloquent words flowed
the green messages of God.

Sometimes,
when there was no need to say anything,
she would write
with her sorrowful looks
upon the eyes
              of all the peoples of the world,
in letters of light,
a thoroughly new chapter
to the Creation of Adam.

In the time of her Advent
it looked as if I had read in her eyes
that the First Created One
was Eve herself,
              not Adam.
God had created her Beautiful
                              and Desirable.
He created her
              as the mirror
of His beauty of meaning.
He wanted to keep her in Paradise forever

in front of his eyes:
free of all sufferings,
untouched by lust,
and like a mirror,
empty of Self,
and brimming with Him.

But God was God,
and His Law is his very Self.
His law is the cipher of life,
the code of existence,
                    in His creatures,
and works as He has willed.
So,
   in His dominion
nothing can remain unchanged forever:

Let us suppose
                that you were the Sun,
what else could be your destiny
but appearing,
            burning bright,
and reaching to the heights of your exhaustion?
And then?
One sun extinguished here,
So that another,
            a new sun,
would appear there,
burning,
        burning bright!

For God,
with His bitter,
            eternal,
                    innate explosions,

Eve was a healing fountain,
giving Him some peace of mind,
some serenity of heart.

So,
      She belonged
to the heavenly paradise
in the Garden of Eden on earth,
where she would have lived forever,
happy,
        and proud,
                    and glowing,
in the all-seeing presence of God.

But God whose Law of Creation
was the same as the Order of Nature,
had no other choice
than to keep Eve in the Garden
like and among other animals
as only one transient link
in the endless chain of Death-and-Birth.

And it was then
                that God Almighty took,
not one of Eve's ribs,
but a handful of the sacred dust
from under her gracious feet
and mixed it with some water
from the river Avdut,
and with it He fashioned the body of Adam,
and breathed into it Life
scented with His own desire for Eve.
With broad shoulders
                    and a heroic chest,

his chest the den of a brave heart,
his heart beating wildly
with insatiable desire for Eve,
taller and much stronger than her,
standing in full height
bowing to her in an eloquent silence,
as if proudly proclaiming:

"I am your humble,
                but unrivalled mate,
Adam,
worthy of keeping your womb happy,
more than capable of fathering your offspring,
and teaching their males
the manners of manliness
and the art of love."

What can we name this game?

This mysterious,
            wonderful,
                     astonishing act of God
in creating Eve
and binding the heart of Adam the Man
to her love
        even at the cost of his death?
Is it the miracle of egoism
With megalomania of self-praising!
But what a beautiful egoism!
What a sweet self-praising!
It so seems
        that this strange God

had always been having
in the very essence of his being
as a concealed power
the possibility of creating the Universe.
And then,
        all of a sudden,
He let this possibility become reality
by a great explosion
in countless galaxies
            scattered in all direction,
eternally in motion,
        burning
            and shining.

Perhaps this game of God
was inspired by Love,
the same Love which is Fire;
the Love whenever it invades my mind,
the tent of Feelings burns out,
and the view of perception darkens.
At a time like this
I close my eyes to the world outside,
I make my obstinate mind
            sit silent in a corner,
and I,
with the ears of my heart,
attentively listen
to the Hoopoe of Vision
relating a new revelation
of an antient mythical legend:

"And Now became Then,
and then,

out from the great explosion
of the concealed possibility
emerged the Infinite Universe,
but only when the chain of the living things
began to appear on Earth
and be settled in themselves,
God could perfectly see and realise
the perfection of His act of Creation:

What had happened was
that the Planet Earth,
through the wonder of His holy breath,
became a blessed womb
eternally pregnant of eternal life.

Then He looked,
with the fervour of love,
at the great chain of life on Earth:
In every single link of the chain
He saw some impressions
      of His great vision,
but in none of them could He see
the comprehensive complex
which He wanted to be
the perfect symbol of His concealed Soul.

So,
from each link of the chain
He chose the component which was,
from the point of view of art
      and aesthetic
the most beautiful one.
Then with all these chosen components,
He made a new living wonder

of sublime beauty and concept,
and called her Eve,
the Mother of Life,
the embodiment of His vision of Creation.

And then,
out of His love for Eve,
which was a reflection
                of his own love for Himself,
He made a mate for her
with the dust of the ground,
and called him Adam,
naïve,
        but arrogant by nature,
his slavish duty
sitting at her feet,
wanting her,
        adoring her,
and worshipping her,
worshipping Eve,
that is worshipping God,
with all his heart and soul.

It was then that Adam,
impassioned with the love of Eve,
came to feel that the shining Sun
gets all its heat and light
from his heart,
and the blue sky
owes its expanse and mirth
                        to his breath.
He came to feel that the whole firmament
with its countless galaxies
                        revolves
not above his head,

but inside the infinite space of his head.
He came to feel
that he wanted to praise Eve,
to adore her,
to worship her
with the passion of Love,
in the light of God,
while praising,
                adoring,
                              worshipping God
in the presence of Eve;
and that is how Poetry was created.

And it was then that Adam
became a "Poet" in his vision and expression
and recited "Songs" in praise of Eve,
and filled with the anxiety of "Reverential Awe"
worshipped God with "Hymns".

It was then that "Faith"
and "love" mixed together
in the peaceful heart of Adam,
and Adam,
            this Wayward Planet,
swaying between "Doubt" and "Certainty,"
in the kingdom of "Divinity",
remained a wanderer,
            an adorer of Eve,
                      and a seeker of God.

London – Written in Persian October 2012 – in English December 2017

Mahmud Kianush

At the Green Gate
For my sisters, Mahboubeh,
Homa and Maryam

The man saw an angel
Standing by a road sign
With two opposing arrows,
                  one red, one green,
On a black pole,
In the middle of a white emptiness.

"Excuse me," he said
                  and paused,
Looking around
              into the white void;
And then,   he asked the angel,
 Could you tell me, please,
"Which of these arrows
                  points to Hell?"

The angel smiled with surprise
                        and said:
"But as far as I know
You must mean Paradise!
Don't you,
        Sir Poet?"

He shook his head,
And,
      with absolute certainty,
                      said:
"No,
I know what I want to say,
                  Lady Angel!

Here,
> in this very situation,
If I am not dreaming,
If I have not lost my mind,
And if this is the World of Afterlife,
Then,
> my whole life
>> has been
A long evidence of sins
For which
> I must be condemned to Hell.

Now the angel began to laugh
And said in good humour:
"Well, Sir Poet,
If you insist to go to Hell,
Follow the green arrow;
It will take you there.
Fare thee well!"

The moment the man's eyes fell
On the shining green arrow,
He was lifted up in the air,
As if riding on the back
Of an invisible,
> gentle,
>> flying horse.

In a blink of the eyes
> he was there,
Dismounting,
> in front of

                    a huge green gate,
Set within the golden walls
                            of Paradise.

To his astonishment,
He saw the same angel
                    standing,
With a friendly
                cheerful smile,
By the small silver door
                        of the gate.
"You are welcome,
                Sir, Poet!
She said,
"We have been waiting for you."

It was beyond his understanding.
"What is happening here!
He said to himself,
"Are they playing with me?
"Is she the same angel,
Or do all the angels look alike?"

Now the small silver door
Opened gently,
                noiselessly.
                        by itself,
And the angel,
Seeing him still silent,
                    bewildered,
And somewhat
                dismayed,

Opened a small blue book
                         and said,
In a very serious,
             but loving tone:

"Our dear Poet,
Now,
       I pray you,
            listen
With your usual interest and respect
To what I am going
                to read to you,
Before entering the Garden of Eternity!"

The man found himself
                     compelled to listen,
And the angel began reading,
With, surprisingly,
               the fatherly tenor voice
Of a man of love and wisdom:

"Verily,
       amongst you,
Only those few deserve
               to be known
As made in my image
Who have in their minds
The right image for my essence;
And who have in their hearts
A pure shrine for my light;
Those who create,
Who create beauty with shapes,
Beauty with colours,
Beauty with sounds,
Beauty with words,

Beauty with meanings;
Those who create
                beauties
                          for pleasure,
Who create pleasure for life;
Those who think,
                discover,
                          and invent,
To preserve and protect life;
Those who love life for its truth,
Those who love truth for its glory,
Those who enjoy glory for love,
Those who enjoy love
                in their search for truth,
Those who want to know themselves,
Because they themselves
                are the Truth,
Because they want to become me,
Because I am the Ultimate Truth,
I am the Light,
I am the Life,
I am the Universe;
And you,
        who are
                one of those few,
 Are gladly welcome
To my Mansion
            of Mysteries.
Let the Forces of Falsehood,
The Forces of Death and Destruction
Be forgotten
            In the Dark of Nothingness!"

And now the angel closed
                the blue book,
And looked at the man
And gave a shining smile!
It was a mid-spring dawn.

The man opened his eyes
And said to himself:
"Another poetical dream!"
And gave a smile of bliss.

London – 6 May 2012

Mahmud Kianush

What Do We Think of the Birds?

Birds are such wonderful angels
that I can watch the show
                    of their real life,
with God at my side,
                    for eternity.
But
in the absence of
                    a winged cosmic self,
– which would desert us forever
if it is left neglected for too long –
we are apt to think of birds
as blessed, happy creatures
that enjoy real freedom,
because they have wings,
because they can fly.

London – 7 June 2018

Her Words

Walking along in a grassland,
she bends down
              every now and then,
and picks a few blades of grass,
which she holds together
between her Musical Fingers,
and looks at them
              with her Hearing Eyes:

It is not hesitation,
nor is it the silent wait
              for inspiration:
The Window of Light
              is gently opening
to the Cosmic Sphere of Mind,
for simply the Great Event
              in which,
                    and how,
a few blades of Grass are turned
into a new,
              unheard,
but exquisite,
           delightful
                    Flower.

13 June 2018

Mahmud Kianush

And He Will Die With Me

I was walking home,
                as usual,
with the help of one strong stick,
but
in a sudden hesitation
                of my right foot
and the failure of the left
                in becoming alert in time,
I staggered,
        luckily,
               towards the wall
which did not break my unruly head,
but actually advised me
in a banging utterance of reproach
that for me
one walking stick,
                no matter how strong,
is not enough anymore!

Now a soft-hearted passer-by
came to me with a consoling face,
thanking God on my behalf
for saving me from a fatal fall.

Oh!
      how I wished he knew
that God was walking with me
with one strong stick
and,
      as the wall advised Him,
He needs one more walking stick,

before the time comes
for His ultimate,
                inevitable fall.

I simply said,
to the benevolent passerby
with a naive,
                imbecile smile:
"God was born with me,
Has been suffering with me,
And verily will die with me!"

London – 17 August 2018

Ode to the Truth of Being Human

One: Songs of Praise

i

There is no need to swear * O you, the Child of Nature, created by God, re-created by yourself * May your aloneness be blessed for you, and your wanderings unending, and your quests everlasting * Your animal self, captive to your sapient self; your sapient self, in conflict with your human self; and your human self, a helpless, tired image, fallen from the empyrean sphere of concepts down to the lowly plane of reality * I praise your Human Self *

ii

There is no need to swear * In your aloneness you are with all; in your wanderings you attain contentment; in your quest you find your meaning * Without you nothing exists, because by naming everything you have re-created everything * Through you everything has obtained meaning; you are the meaning of everything * I praise your Human Self *

iii

There is no need to swear * Before you the Earth had revolved around the Sun for thousands of million years and neither of them was aware * Before your arrival there was no sky up there, and there will not be any after your departure * The Sky is your eyes when you are looking up above your head, in the absolute absence of aboveness and belowness * I praise your Human Self *

iv

There is no need to swear ∗ Let every one of the existing galaxies, give birth, moment by moment, to a thousand new ones; they will be seen as some new ways drawn with spilt milk across the blue carpet of space ∗ Milky Way? What milk? What way? This is poetry emitting from your eyes, reflecting in everything ∗ I praise your Human Self ∗

v

There is no need to swear ∗ Inspired by the movements of the weeping willow branches in the wind, and by the whirling motion of bonfire flames, you let dance flow into your body ∗ You enjoyed listening to the sweet songs of warblers, but when yourself began to sing, the Universe with all its commotion fell silent in astonishment ∗ And then, against the vacuous indifference of Nature to your blind predicament, you began to give voice, through many instruments made of wood, metal and strings, to the primeval melodies suppressed to silence in your resolute, restless heart ∗ I praise your Human Self ∗

vi

There is no need to swear ∗ You look at one of many aquatic animals in a coral reef ∗ Lo, what a wonder! ∗ How can an animal with so mysterious a shape, with all these enigmatic patterns, these harmonious but contrasting colours, be real? ∗ Camouflage? To what end? ∗ In a world where all the predators and preys are preyed on either by each other or, ultimately, by the Mother Earth, camouflages look to you as something absolutely absurd and insipid ∗ You cannot agree with a "survival" which is based only on "struggle", and the "wonder" loses all its "glory" ∗ I praise your Human Self ∗

vii

There is no need to swear ∗ You do observe and understand and appreciate the harmony of lines and shapes in the arrangement of colours and for that matter you admire the art of Nature ∗ But in the art of Nature you do not find your

Meaning, and therefore, you re-create it with your own Meaning ∗ Your Art is not an imitation of Nature, as it has always been said, but it is an answer to Nature, as I have found it ∗ I praise your Human Self ∗

viii

There is no need to swear ∗ After years of contemplation, it was revealed to you that "pleasure" was rather a delusive impulse to persuade you to satisfy the hungry needs of your body, your corporeal being ∗ So, you gave the new name of Love to something that was the hungry need of Sexual Attraction ∗ Thus the Pain of Hunger became the Sorrow of Separation from the Beloved", and the Pleasure of Mating became the Union of Lover and Beloved, and you became the maker of Lyric Love Poems, not the Mute Obedient Slave of Nature ∗ I praise your Human Self ∗

ix

There is no need to swear ∗ Your Animal Self is immortal, because it has no past to afflict him with the malaise of regret, nor has it any future to live in perpetual anxiety out of terror of death ∗ Without knowing consciously, it knows by instinct that the meaning of existence is to be born and to reproduce ∗ And your Sapient Self cannot free himself from the memories of the past, because he always remembers with regrets, and the future frightens him, because it will end up with his forced departure from a world, from the only world which he knows well, which is everything he is ∗ And it is for these reasons that he is never present in his passing life while time is still present ∗ To be born and to reproduce keep his heart warm but do not alleviate the mental pain of his being aware of the transitoriness of life ∗ And this is the time when your Human Self, if your Sapient Self is conscientiously awake and alert, appears in you ∗ And it is this Human Self of yours that opens the mystery of Immortality in a happy eternal moment ∗ I praise your Human Self ∗

x

There is no need to swear ∗ Your Human Self, created by you in your aloneness, somehow, in some happy, eternal moments, puts your Animal Self under a mysterious spell ∗ You separate from your Self ∗ You become free from your Self ∗ You become God in your new Self ∗ You have obtained clemency from your body, your Physical Self ∗ While having roots in the earth, you have taken wing, soaring up to the heavens ∗ With your eyes closed, you have given light to the horizons of vision ∗ And now that the blue firmament with all its stars has become the space of your mind, you meet there the white Dove of Soul ∗ I praise your Human Self ∗

xi

There is no need to swear ∗ In your happy, eternal moments, when you look at something, it becomes beautiful, becomes beauty, becomes your beloved ∗ And in your beloveds you become beautiful, become beauty, become the meaning of Creation ∗ And you embrace the eternity, and in the meaning of your Human Self and of God, you become oblivious of everything else ∗ I praise your Human Self ∗

xii

There is no need to swear ∗ It is a tiny wild flower, with turquoise blue petals and a golden centre, much smaller than a dew drop ∗ You sit down, on the grass, in front of the tiny wild flower and your mind becomes empty of History ∗ The tiny wild flower sticks to your gaze of fascination, becomes your gaze, becomes your eyes, becomes your soul ∗ This happens through your mysterious spell which becomes more effective during your happy eternal moments, while your Animal Self is under your spell ∗ And thus you remain free to see the features of the cosmos in the face of a tiny wild flower, the size of a dewdrop ∗ I praise your Human Self ∗

Two: Songs of Admiration

i

Your aloneness is great * Your Animal Self is bondage to Nature * Your Sapient Self is in bondage to your Animal Self * And you elevate your "self" from the pit of this bondage to the summit of freedom * And there you forgive all the wrongdoings of these two wretched slaves * You avoid complaining about the wrongs they do to you, because they are corrupted by Nature, but you have come into a shining and pure being from the depth of their malicious corruption, as does a beautiful, shining fragrant red rose from the hard and dark heart of the earth * They do not know this, but you know it well, and this makes your aloneness greater * I admire your great aloneness *

ii

Your Sorrow is great * Your Sapient Self is curious, questing and proud * With the ambition of flying through and across the galaxies, lands on the Moon, which seems to be too far away, though in reality it is but a small neighbour to the Earth * The prideful glory of this trivial triumph drives him out of his senses * The potential danger of this conceit makes your Human Self shudder in apprehension, but he finds it almost impossible to prevent him from his disastrous follies * And your Sapient Self who is trying to search the planet Mars inch by inch to find a single drop of water with one unicellular living thing, is turning the vast oceans of the Earth into hells of pollution and death for their myriads of beautiful and astonishing animals and plants, and turns the heavenly paradise of the Earth into deadly deserts * And this makes your sorrow greater * I admire your great sorrow *

iii

Your despair is great * In deep astonishment, you lay your head on your knees and addressing your Sapient Self, but as if wanting your own heart to hear, you say:

"We are told that there are hundreds of thousands of millions of stars in our galaxy alone * Our Sun and her planets and moons are a group of outcast islands, flung far away from their continent of the Milky Way, into the ocean of space * Only in this galaxy there must be one hundred thousand million suns. Then the suns of the Universe are infinite in their numbers * And all these suns must have their own planets and moons * Suppose that our sun, as the begetter of a planet like Earth, with life in such abundance and diversity, is absolutely unique among all the suns of the Universe * If this be the case, then the Earth must be the one and only living planet in the whole infinite Universe * O you, my Sapient Self, give a careful pause to your insane passion of haste! With the annihilation of life on earth the existence of the Existence will sink into eternal oblivion * Do not let God's feelings get injured in me" *

And because you know that your Sapient Self is intoxicated with self-deception, this fact makes your despair greater * I admire your great sorrow *

iv

Your anger is great * With its flameless fire it can burn the whole universe into ashes in your mind and scatter the ashes in the sphere of your heart * What ignites your anger is the ignorance of your Sapient Self and it burns you, because Knowledge is Light and light is achieved by burning * And you know that your Sapient Self is not incapable of knowing, but his Animal Self, perhaps quite unintentionally, acts as an obstacle to his will * And it is this Sapient Self of yours that surrenders all his sapientness, all his intelligence, his powers of invention, discovery and initiative, the glory of his thought, the beauty of his imagination, and his divine love to the natural needs of his Animal Self * And how strange that he, your Sapient Self, thinks that he is the commanding master of his Animal Self * And it is this arrogant bold ignorance of his that makes your anger greater * I admire your great anger *

V

And your Joy is also great * You know that you have not come into being by yourself * And you know that you are here without the request and consent of your free will * And you know that you are a single part of a great complicated whole whose other parts may not be aware of their beingness * And you do not know why you are here. And you do not know who wanted you to be here * But it is a solemn fact and quite obvious to you that you have suddenly appeared here out of a handful of dust and a bucketful of water by the life-giving Bang of the Big mystery to rise up and begin your wondering restlessness of bewilderment * That is why, with all the toils and tortures and pains of living, your rejoice of life is greater than your aloneness * Your rejoice is greater than your sorrows * Your rejoice is greater than your despairs * Your rejoice is greater than your anger * Because you see yourself, not in a handful of dust and a bucketful of water, but as a mysterious, unnatural, unworldly, unexpected, unprophecizable miracle, risen above the absurdity of its origin, that gives a shining clear meaning to the whole infinite Universe * I admire your rejoice, O the Human Self of the Sapient Self of the Animal Self of Man! * Live and rejoice! * Vivet, et exultate! *

About the poet

Mahmud Kianush was born in 1934 in Mashhad, in the north-east of Iran. His family moved to Tehran when he was about 12 years old. At this age he began writing poems, mostly *ghazal*, a classical Persian form similar in some aspects to English odes and sonnets. In high school, when he was about 16, having already read the works of some European writers in Persian translation, he was encouraged to write short stories and his first story, published in the "National Students Organisation Weekly," won a national prize. Later, while still in high school, his short stories were published, under different pen names, in leading literary weeklies. One of these weeklies was *The Third Force, Literary Weekly* whose editor, Jalal Al-e Ahmad, had assumed the stories sent by post to him were written by a writer of his own age and level.

After studying for two years in the Teachers Training School in Tehran, Mahmud Kianush began teaching in elementary schools. At that time he was nineteen and while teaching, he attended Tehran University and received a Bachelor of Arts degree in English language and literature. In his first year in the university, he published his Persian translation of John Steinbeck's novel, *To A God Unknown*.

It was at this time that he began writing modern poems, using a form similar to "free verse," but this kind of freedom in style did not satisfy his search for aesthetic innovations and soon he returned to metrical poetry, developing new rhythms on the basis of the classical ones, making them for different subjects in accordance with their musical reflections in his mind. He used the same metre throughout a poem, but with lines of different lengths and with new arrangements of rhymes, in harmony with the images and meanings.

His contributions of poems, short stories, essays and translations to the leading literary magazines and periodicals soon made him famous enough to be invited to undertake the editorship of the most prestigious literary monthly, *Sokhan* (Word). After four years, he resigned from this literary post and devoted all his time to writing. However, he was then invited by the Department of Educational Publications in the Ministry of Education, to examine the situation of children's poetry in relation to their five biweekly magazines which were published for students of elementary and secondary schools. What he found was that the few poets who wrote for children thought that versifying educational and moral subjects in a simple, childish language was the only way of writing poems for children. Feeling that it was his national duty to do something about these cultural shortcomings, he began writing real poetry for children. During his eight years of contributing to these magazines, he derived certain principles from his own experience and wrote a book about children's poetry. Later this book became a manual for the poets who wanted to write for children. To this day his poems are imitated by many poets who write for children.

Kianush collected and published his poems for children and young adults in eight books, all of which won different awards. He became known as the founder of children's poetry in Iran. But he does not care for this title which he believes to be quite contrary to his real achievement as the messenger of the truth hidden in the heart of perceptible realities which, in occasional blessed moments, reveals itself to him on the horizon of artistic beauty. He says that in Iran, a country where the people, especially the intelligentsia, have since the late nineteenth century been possessed by the politics of freedom and social change, the popularity of a poet depends on his being the artistic mouthpiece and interpreter of the political aspirations of the populace. On the other hand, a poet like himself, one of the few poets who have not sacrificed the universal principles of the art of poetry for the pleasure of temporal popularity, is considered difficult, obscure, elitist, philosophical, idealist, and so forth.

Poetry for Mahmud Kianush is the language of the childhood of 'historical man'. He believes that the first human beings began to understand themselves, the world around them and the mysteries of the universe by their poetical interpretations of everything they saw and felt, and this is what real poets have always done and will always do. He agrees with the ancient idea that "man is a political animal," but he adds that man must remain faithful to his primordial nature and first be a poet.

In 1974, Kianush who, as a civil servant in Iran, was an advisor to the Secretary of State for Administration and Employment Affairs in managerial and training publications, asked for early retirement, and in 1976, with his wife and two children, moved to London. For thirty-four years he worked for the Persian Section of the BBC, as a freelance producer of literary, cultural, and sociological, as well as bilingual English teaching programmes.

Mahmud Kianush has published fourteen books of poems, five collection of short stories, seven novels, two plays and eight books of literary criticism and several collections of essays of social philosophy and criticism. For children and young adults he has published five books of stories and eight books of poems.

He has also translated and published works by John Steinbeck, D. H. Lawrence, Eugene O'Neill, Aimé Cesaire, Samuel Beckett, Athol Fugard, Par Lagerkvist, Federico Garcia Lorca, Konstantin Cavafy, and others. He has a variety of other books published on the internet (among them five of satirical poems), but none of these has any chance of passing through the censorship in Iran. He edited and translated the anthology, *Modern Persian Poetry* (Rockingham Press, 1996), including the works of poets ranging from Nima Yushij (b. 1895) to those born in the 1960s. The first book of his own English poems, *Of Birds and Men: Poems from a Persian Divan*, was published by Rockingham Press in 2004. His English translation of one of his books, *Through the Window of the Taj Mahal*, was also published by Rockingham Press in 2007. In 2010 a bilingual (Persian-English) selection of his poems, *Thorns and Pearls* (Khaar-o Morvaarid), was published in Tehran by Ghatreh Publications, and in 2011 a collection of his poems, entitled *The Amber Shell of Self* was published by Rockingham Press. His next book of new poems, published by Rockingham Press in 2012 was *The Songs of Man*. His latest book of poems published by Rockingham Press in 2014 was *Poems of the Living Present*. His last book of English poems is *The Journey and Other Poems*.

Lightning Source UK Ltd.
Milton Keynes UK
UKHW010657221020
372026UK00001B/60